For Ma and Pa   Love, Mels.

OXFORD
UNIVERSITY PRESS

Great Clarendon Street, Oxford OX2 6DP

Oxford University Press is a department of the University of Oxford.
It furthers the University's objective of excellence in research, scholarship,
and education by publishing worldwide in

Oxford New York

Auckland Bangkok Buenos Aires Cape Town Chennai
Dar es Salaam Delhi Hong Kong Istanbul Karachi Kolkata
Kuala Lumpur Madrid Melbourne Mexico City Mumbai Nairobi
São Paulo Shanghai Singapore Taipei Tokyo Toronto

Oxford is a registered trade mark of Oxford University Press
in the UK and in certain other countries

This selection and arrangement © John Foster 2002

The moral rights of the author have been asserted

Database right Oxford University Press (maker)

British Library Cataloguing in Publication Data available

ISBN 0192762710 Hardback
ISBN 0192762729 Paperback

1 3 5 7 9 10 8 6 4 2

Typeset in Bembo/Twinkle
Printed in Singapore

Acknowledgements: **Gwenda Black**: 'Tree Bear', copyright © Gwenda Black, reproduced by kind permission of Ewan and Ceri Black. **Alan Bold**: 'Lullaby', copyright © Alan Bold 1984, first published in John Foster (ed): A Very F
Poetry Book (OUP, 1984), reprinted by permission of Alice Bold. **Charles Causley**: 'Climb the Stair' from All Day Saturday (Macmillan), reprinted by permission of David Higham Associates. **Gina Douthwaite**: 'Baby in a Basket',
published as 'Lullaby' in John Foster (ed): My First Oxford Book of Poems (OUP, 2000), reprinted by permission of the author. **Olive Dove**: 'How Far' first published in Poetry Corner (BBC, 1981), reprinted by permission of Mrs
Dean. **Eleanor Farjeon**: 'Good Night' from Silver Sand and Snow (Michael Joseph), reprinted by permission of David Higham Associates. **John Foster**: 'Night Time', copyright © John Foster 1999, first published in Bare Bear and
Other Rhymes (OUP), and 'Lullaby', copyright © John Foster 2002, first published in this collection, both by permission of the author. **Lee Bennett Hopkins**: 'Night Bear', copyright © Lee Bennett Hopkins 1972, from Surprises
selected by Lee Bennett Hopkins (Harper Collins Publishers, 1972), reprinted by permission of Curtis Brown, Ltd, New York. **Elizabeth Jennings**: 'Lullaby' from The Secret Brother (Macmillan, 1966), reprinted by permission of
David Higham Associates. **Jean Kenward**: 'Night Light', copyright © Jean Kenward 1991, first published in John Foster (ed): Night Poems (OUP, 1991), reprinted by permission of the author. **Dennis Lee**: 'Good Night, Good Nigh
from Jelly Belly (Macmillan of Canada, 1983), copyright © Dennis Lee 1983, reprinted by permission of Westwood Creative Artists on behalf of the author. **Eve Merriam**: 'You be Saucer' from You Be Good & I'll Be Night (Morr
Jr Books, 1988), copyright © Eve Merriam 1988, reprinted by permission of Marian Reiner on behalf of the author. **Sarojini Naidu**: 'Cradle Song' from Indo-English Poetry in Bengal edited by K C Lahiri (OUP, 1945), copyright
holder not traced. **James Reeves**: 'Time to Go Home' from Complete Poems for Children (Heinemann, 1973), reprinted by permission of Laura Cecil on behalf of the James Reeves Estate. **Barrie Wade**: 'Lullaby' from Rainbow
(OUP, 1995), reprinted by permission of the author. **Clyde Watson**: 'Hushabye My Darling', copyright © Clyde Watson 1978, from Catch Me and Kiss Me and Say It Again (Wm Collins Sons & Co, 1978), reprinted by permission
Curtis Brown, Ltd, New York.

Although we have tried to trace and contact all copyright holders, this has not been possible in one case. If notified the publishers will be pleased to rectify any errors or omissions at the earliest opportunity.

Drift Upon a Dream

Poems for sleepy babies

chosen by John Foster

illustrated by

Melanie Williamson

OXFORD
UNIVERSITY PRESS

The Evening is Coming

The evening is coming.
The sun sinks to rest.
The birds are all flying
straight home to their nests.
'Caw, caw,' says the crow
as he flies overhead.
It's time little children
were going to bed.

Here comes the pony.
His work is all done.
Down through the meadow
he takes a good run.
Up go his heels,
and down goes his head.
It's time little children
were going to bed.

Anon.

Night-time

The sun has slipped behind the hill.
The flowers' petals are closed and still.
The birds in the trees are silent now
As they softly settle upon the bough.
In his basket the dog breathes deep,
Puts his head on his paws and falls asleep.

John Foster

Climb the Stair

Climb the stair, Katie,
Climb the stair, Paul,
The sun is down
On the orchard wall.

All through the valley
The air turns blue,
Silvers the meadow-grass
With dew.

High in the tower
The scritch-owl cries,
Watching where darkest
Darkness lies.

The bats round the barnyard
Skim and stray
From last of light
To first of day.

Unseen, the water
Winds on the weir
Sings a night-song
For all to hear.

Goodnight, Katie,
Goodnight, Paul,
Sleep till the new day
Comes to call.

Charles Causley

You be Saucer

You be saucer,
I'll be cup,
piggyback, piggyback,
pick me up.

You be tree,
I'll be pears,
carry me, carry me
up the stairs.

You be Good,
I'll be Night,
tuck me in, tuck me in
nice and tight.

Eve Merriam

Teddy Bear, Teddy Bear

Teddy Bear, Teddy Bear, turn around.
Teddy Bear, Teddy Bear, touch the ground.
Teddy Bear, Teddy Bear, show your shoe.
Teddy Bear, Teddy Bear, that will do.

Teddy Bear, Teddy Bear, go upstairs.
Teddy Bear, Teddy Bear, say your prayers.
Teddy Bear, Teddy Bear, turn out the light.
Teddy Bear, Teddy Bear, say goodnight.

Traditional

Tree Bear

Listen to the tree bear
Crying in the night
Crying for his mammy
In the pale moonlight.

What will his mammy do
When she hears him cry?
She'll tuck him in a cocoa-pod
And sing a lullaby.

Gwenda Black

Night Bear

In the dark of night
   when all is still
and I'm half-sleeping in my bed:

It's good to know
   my teddy-bear
is snuggling at my head.

Lee Bennett Hopkins

Star Light

Star light, star bright,
First star I see tonight,
I wish I may, I wish I might,
Have the wish I wish tonight.

Anon.

Lullaby

The stars have switched their lights on.
Day's curtains have been drawn.
The birds are resting in the trees.
There's dew upon the lawn.

The toys are in their boxes.
The stories have been read.
It's time for drifting off to sleep
Tucked safely up in bed.

John Foster

Rock-a-bye, Baby

Rock-a-bye, baby,
Thy cradle is green.
Father's a nobleman,
Mother's a queen;
And Betty's a lady
And wears a gold ring;
And Johnny's a drummer
And drums for the king.

Traditional

Hush, Little Baby, Don't Say a Word

Hush, little baby, don't say a word,
Papa's gonna buy you a mocking-bird.

And if that mocking-bird won't sing,
Papa's gonna buy you a diamond ring.

If that diamond ring turns to brass,
Papa's gonna buy you a looking-glass.

If that looking-glass gets broke,
Papa's gonna buy you a billy goat.

And if that billy goat falls down,
You'll still be the sweetest little baby in town.

Traditional Afro-American

How Far

'How far away
Is the evening star?'
'Ask the night horse,
He knows how far.

Talk to him gently.
Give him honey and hay,
Seven bells for his bridle
And he'll take you away.

Snorting white fire
He will stream through the air
Past mountains of the moon
And the rainbow's stair.

And if you go singing
Through the dark and the cold
Your purse will be filled
With silver and gold.'

Olive Dove

Cradle Song

From groves of spice
O'er fields of rice
Athwart the lotus-stream
   I bring for you
   Aglint with dew
A little lovely dream.

Sweet, shut your eyes
The wild fire-flies
Dance through the fairy neem:
   From the poppy-bole
   For you I stole
A little lovely dream.

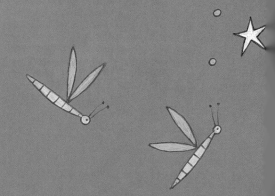

Dear eyes, goodnight,
In golden light
The stars around you gleam;
   On you I press
   With soft caress
A little lovely dream.

Sarojini Naidu

Goodnight

Now goodnight.
Fold up your clothes
As you were taught,
Fold your two hands,
Fold up your thought;
Day is the plough-land,
Night is the stream,
Day is for doing
And night is for dream.
Now goodnight.

Eleanor Farjeon

Baby in a Basket

Baby in a basket
floats upon a stream,
rocks along the river
of a gentle dream,

sails away in slumber
on a cot of rushes
where the lapping of water
soothes and hushes.

Baby in a basket
floats upon a stream,
rocks along the river
of a gentle dream.

Gina Douthwaite

Sandmen, Sandmen

Sandmen, sandmen,
Wise and creepy,
Croon dream songs
To make us sleepy.

A lovely maid with deep dark eyes
Is queen of all their lullabies.
On her ancient moon-guitar
She strums a sleep-song to a star;
And when the deep dark shadows fall
Snow-white lilies hear her call.

Sandmen, sandmen,
Wise and creepy,
Croon dream-songs
To make us sleepy.

Anon.

Hushabye, My Darling

Hushabye, my darling
Don't you make a peep,
Little creatures everywhere
Are settling down to sleep.

Fishes in the millpond
Goslings in the barn
Kitten by the fireside
Baby in my arms.

Listen to the raindrops
Singing you to sleep,
Hushabye, my darling
Don't you make a peep.

Clyde Watson

African Lullaby

Sleep, my little one! The night is all wind and rain;
The meal has been wet by the raindrops
　　and bent is the sugarcane;
O Giver who gives to the people,
　　in safety my little son keep!
My little son with the head-dress,
　　sleep, sleep, sleep!

Traditional African

Lullaby

Close your eyes gently
  And cuddle in
Keep yourself snug, a
  New day will begin.

Have pleasant dreams about
  Those things you love,
Sleep is an island
  Waiting above.

Night is a blanket
  Keeping you warm
If you close eyes you can
  Come to no harm.

Dreams are like journeys
  Drifting along,
Rest is a present
  Keeping you strong.

Alan Bold

Lullaby

Hush, can you hear
in the thickening deep
the air in the trees
is falling asleep?

Hush, can you see
where the darkening skies
stretch over the sunset
and close heavy eyes?

Hush, can you hear
where the whispering corn
is settling down
and starting to yawn?

Hush, can you see
in the moon's silver beam
the light of the world
beginning to dream?

Hush, can you feel
the whole world give a sigh
and fall fast asleep
to your lullaby?

Barrie Wade

Sweet and Low

Sweet and low, sweet and low,
Wind of the western sea,
Low, low, breathe and blow,
Wind of the western sea!
Over the rolling waters go,
Come from the dying moon, and blow,
Blow him again to me;
While, my little one, while my pretty one sleeps.

Sleep and rest, sleep and rest,
Father will come to thee soon;
Rest, rest, on mother's breast,
Father will come to thee soon;
Father will come to his babe in the nest,
Silver sails all out of the west
Under the silver moon;
Sleep, my little one, sleep, my pretty one, sleep.

Alfred, Lord Tennyson